THE GRAND HORSE SHOW

Written by: *Camille Hourtane*
Illustrations: *Anastasia Rybalka*

Bleu RUBIS

At **Bleu Rubis Publishing**, our mission is to create fun and educational books to help children shine.

We have lots of projects and we're just starting our adventure!

To help us improve, we invite parents to leave a review on the Amazon product page.

THANK YOU!

Your opinion **matters.**

WELCOME TO THE ADVENTURE!

Young rider, here you are at the beginning of an incredible horse-filled adventure. You will soon enter the **Little Gallop Equestrian Center** and take your first steps into the world of horseback riding.

Throughout your adventure, you'll need to care for horses, but also become friends with them, so you can ride them and take them to competition. If you want, you can also give them medical attention: but before that, you'll need to perfect your knowledge and earn the veterinarian's confidence.

Budding rider, you shouldn't think this adventure will be a walk in the park! Horses are complex animals and you'll have to work hard, train regularly, and be humble to earn their trust. **Never forget about your horse's well-being.** This is the only way to become its best friend and form an unbreakable bond.

IT'S YOUR TURN!

You'll begin your adventure at 1, when you're not yet a member of the Little Gallop Equestrian Center. Then you'll train, prove yourself, and become a real horseback rider. A few rules for a fantastic adventure:

Make Your Own Choices

At the end of each chapter, you will have a choice to make. Depending on your choice, you will turn to the chapter number listed. Caution: Your choices will have consequences! The consequences will become greater as you continue your adventure, so think carefully…

Score Points

As you read, you will be able to earn points ★. Keep track of these points in Chapter 43 so you won't forget. The goal of the game is to score as many points as possible. To do this, you can either:

Reach the end of the adventure. There are 12 different endings: 9 defeats and 3 victories. Defeat earns you ★5 points and victory earns you ★20.

Complete the activities. Each activity earns you ★3 points. You'll find the solutions in Chapter 45.

Answer the questions in Chapter 42. To help you answer correctly, read all the "Did you know?" sections throughout your adventure to learn more about horses. Each correct answer in 42 will earn you ★3 points. You can check your answers in 45.

Let yourself follow your path – everything will be explained! There's only one thing to remember: to score every point, you have to **read everything**, discover **every ending**, and complete **every activity**.

LET THE ADVENTURE BEGIN!

1 Howdy, young rider! Welcome to the Little Gallop Equestrian Center. It's a family stable that loves to take care of its horses and its riders. Here is where you will begin to discover the wonderful world of horseback riding. You'll be able to learn new things and test your knowledge, meet the Center's employees and horses, and take part in fantastic adventures. Many careers revolve around horses, and many paths are open to you. But be aware, you must always remember: whatever direction you choose, your horse's well-being is the most important thing.

To start your adventure, choose which section of the Equestrian Center you'd like to visit first.

To visit the stables, go to 22.

To visit the jumping course, turn to 9.

IT'S YOUR TURN!

Earn 3 points

Test your horseback riding vocabulary. Fill in the following crossword grid:

1 → The person who mounts a horse
2 → What's attached under a horse's hoof
3 → What comes after a trot
4 → Metal piece that goes inside the horse's mouth to steer it
5 → Where you take a horseback riding lesson
6 → Where the rider puts their foot
7 → The top of the horse's mane, on its forehead
8 → Faster than a walk
9 → One of horses' favorite foods
10 → What you call a horse with a reddish-brown coat

2 Dr. Carol, the veterinarian, arrives. A veterinarian has to come to the stables at least two to four times per year, to check on the general health of the horses, make sure their vaccines are up to date, and administer deworming medicine. Deworming helps prevent the horses from catching intestinal parasites. The veterinarian can also be called in at any time if there is an injury or sickness.

When you see Dr. Carol enter Saffron's stall to check on him, you ask if you can help her. Over her glasses, she looks you up and down with a serious expression. Then, she turns to Alex and asks him if he thinks you have what it takes to be a veterinarian.

If you helped Alex clean Saffron's wound, go to 38.

If you didn't help Alex, turn to 4.

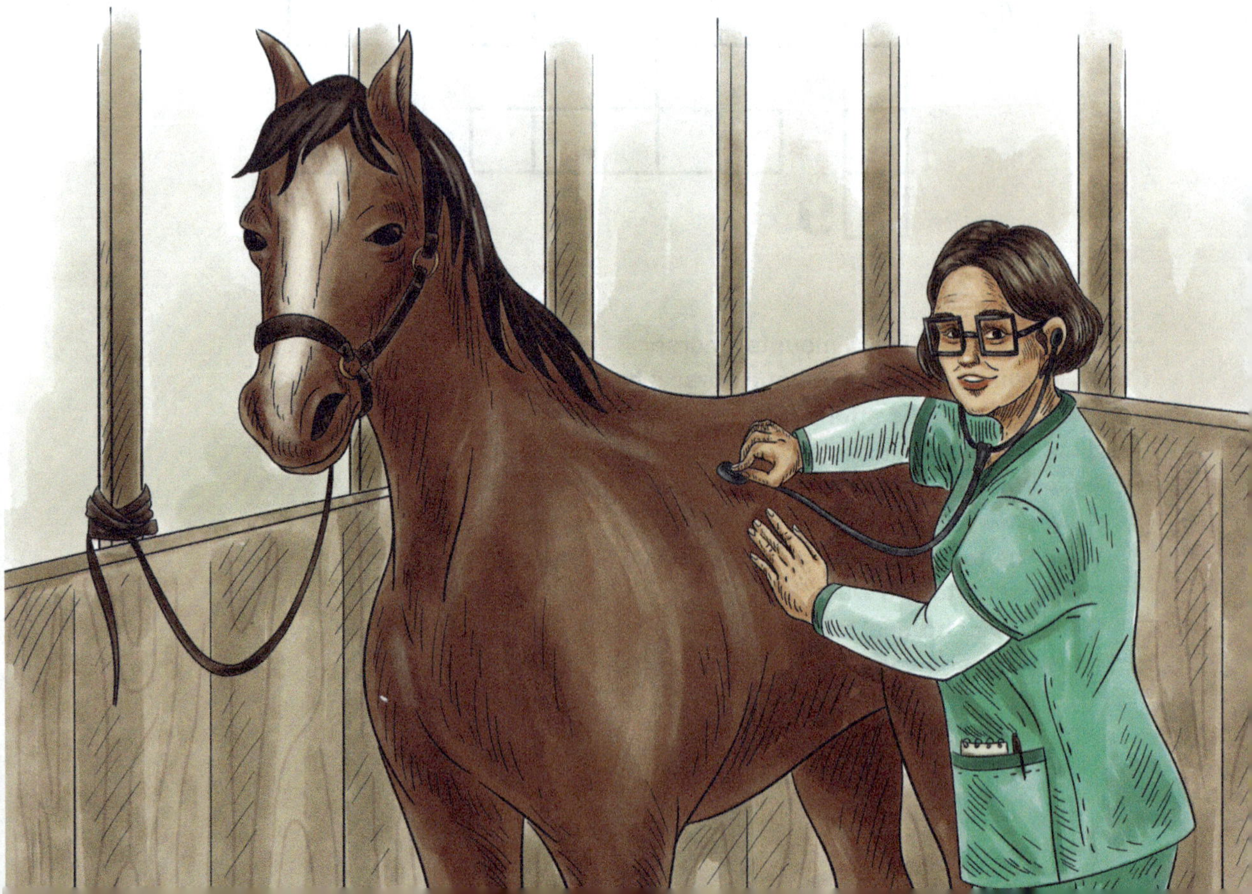

3 Big news: The circus is in town! You're already picturing the big red and yellow tent, the trapeze artists flying through the air, the tightrope walkers crossing a wire at dizzying heights, clowns in colorful makeup making the whole crowd laugh. You also imagine the riders dancing on horseback, the fire-breathers, the knife-throwers, the magicians with their sleight of hand, and the acrobats that seem to defy gravity.

Mr. Loyal, the ringmaster, drives through the streets in a little car, announcing that a parade will take place this afternoon. However, you haven't yet finishing reading your book.

Will you go to the parade, or would you rather finish your reading?

Go watch the parade

Study your books

Then continue to 40.

4

A veterinary career is difficult and requires years of study, but it's also interesting and allows you to spend time with animals every day.
You need a lot of heart, a lot of patience, and a lot of determination to be a good veterinarian.
Unfortunately, when you had the chance to help Alex treat Saffron, you chose instead to go see the other horses. It's a pity, because grooms often know a lot about a stable's horses, and they have a good understanding of how to care for them. You could have learned a lot from Alex.

Dr. Carol turns down your offer of help. Next time, be more serious about learning: horses are complex animals. You need to understand them before you can take care of them.

You still earn 5 *points.*

Restart your adventure. Go back to 1.

IT'S YOUR TURN!

Earn 3 *points*

Complete the Sudoku grid below. The rule is that each symbol (, , , , ,) must be used once - and only once - in each row, column, and rectangle of 6 boxes.

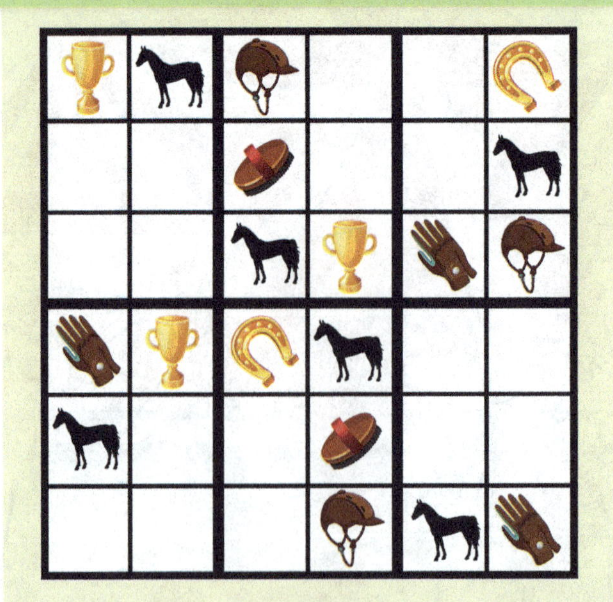

5 Saffron's leg is healing well and he'll soon be able to do lessons again. Dr. Carol sees that you did a good job cleaning the wound. She prescribes an antiseptic cream to apply twice a day for five days, and she shows you how to apply it.

She also checks in on Tornado, a horse with allergies. She explains to you how to administer a shot of medicine. By following the doctor's instructions and speaking softly, you're able to reassure Tornado.

Dr. Carol is rarely impressed. However, your serious attitude, your listening, and your relationship with the horses demands respect. She has a very high opinion of you and suggests that you become her assistant.

If you want to become Dr. Carol's assistant, turn to 7.

If you'd rather go horseback riding, go to 31.

6 You stroke Chocolate's neck, then you scratch his withers. Chocolate really appreciates it. The withers is a spot that a horse can't reach on his own. When they're out in the pasture, two horses will reach past each other's heads and scratch one another's withers. It's a sign of affection.

Alex, the groom, is impressed with how you went about approaching Chocolate. He thinks you have a lot of sensitivity when it comes to horses, so he offers to teach you how to become a horse whisperer, once he has finished cleaning the stables.

If you want to become a horse whisperer, you can wait for Alex to finish cleaning the stables or you can choose to help him.

Help Alex ***Play with the other horses while you wait***

Then continue to 18.

If you'd rather go horseback riding, turn to 31.

7 You have now become Dr. Carol's assistant. You accompany her on a regular basis as she visits her clients. Sometimes you care for cats, dogs, or other pets. Other times, you go to different stables or farms and care for horses, cows, donkeys, goats, and sheep. It's hard work, but very rewarding. You have a great touch when it comes to animals, and you help them stay calm during their check-ups. You've also learned how to bandage, to clean different types of wounds, and to give medicine.
Dr. Carol gives you books to read to perfect your knowledge. It's very important that you study, especially if you want to become a veterinarian. The more you know, the better you'll be able to treat sick and injured animals.

Continue to 3.

DID YOU KNOW?
There are around 350 species of horses and ponies.

8 The day of the national competition has arrived. Lots of riders and horses have come. It's a bustling scene. People are running all over the place to saddle their mounts, get their competition bibs, or find a replacement girth or brushing boot. The commentators' voices crackle over the loudspeakers, calling out riders' numbers and commenting on their performance. The jumping course is difficult, but the participants' skill level is very high. Many riders complete the course without any mistakes. It's easy to see they've all trained very hard and that they have very good relationships with their horses.

You're nervous, but you want to do your best.

If you haven't become friends with your horse, go to 15.

If you have become friends with your horse, go to 41.

(If you can't remember, check in 44)

9 You arrive at the jumping ring. It's very spacious, and filled with jumps of different styles and colors.

Lisa, the instructor, notices that you're interested in jumping. It's a difficult sport, but very exciting. You need courage, a serious attitude, and a very good relationship with your horse if you want to have a good run. Lisa offers to let you take the entrance exam. If your score is high enough, you'll be able to join the Equestrian Center's jumping class.

Continue to 31.

DID YOU KNOW?

The world record for jumping was set in 1949 by a horse named Huaso. With his rider Alberto Larraguibel, he cleared a jump that was 8 ft 1 in high!

10 Dr. Carol is very satisfied with your commitment. Your dedication to studying your books allowed you to learn a lot about horses and their care. She permits you to come assist her at the birth.
When you arrive at the Equestrian Center, Alex has already tied up the mare's tail to prevent the long hairs from getting in the way. The stall is very large and the bed of straw is very thick. The mare turns in circles for several minutes before lying down. You stay close to her head to stroke her and reassure her, while Dr. Carol makes sure that labor proceeds without any issues.

Fortunately, the birth unfolds as it should. After two hours, a foal is born. Dr. Carol asks you to rub it dry with some straw and help it stand.

Soon the mare stands, and the foal walks over to her for its first drink of milk. Congratulations! You've been such great help to Alex and Dr. Carol. Thanks to you, Cinnamon has brought a magnificent little foal into the world.

You earn 20 *points.*

But you can restart your adventure at 1 *.*

11 You work with your horse every day. You practice jumping, but also strength and posture, dressage, and trail rides, because these other areas help to improve communication, control, and endurance. You train hard and you make great progress.

The instructor is impressed with your dedication. She explains to you that the Equestrian Center's jumping competition is coming up. The winner qualifies for the national competition. Thanks to your training, Lisa thinks you're good enough to compete in two weeks and she signs you up.

If you want to go buy a new outfit for the competition, go shopping in 19.

If you would rather stay and train with your horse, turn to 39.

12 Dr. Carol, the veterinarian who works with the Little Gallop Equestrian Center, visits Chocolate for a check-up. She is concerned, because he's not eating enough and he's losing weight. She gives him vitamins to improve his energy.
However, the problem is not physical, but emotional. Chocolate is depressed – that's why he's not eating. He needs someone to take care of him and lift his spirits, or he could fall seriously ill. Mental health is just as important as physical well-being, for both humans and horses. You have to take care of both body and mind. The only way for Chocolate to get better is to make him happy again.

If you want to work with Dr. Carol to treat sick and injured animals, go to 7.

If you'd rather help Chocolate feel better, turn to 21.

13 You take a sleeping bag and pillow to share Chocolate's stall with him. This way, he won't be alone anymore and he'll always have company. When you talk with Alex about this, he says it's a bad idea. Chocolate needs a friend, but he also needs his space. He clearly demonstrated that the first time you entered his stall. Being with him constantly would make him feel overwhelmed and would risk stressing him out. This is not a good solution to help make him happy again.

You didn't listen to Alex's advice and you didn't respect the signals Chocolate was sending. You haven't acted like a horse whisperer.

You still earn 5 *points.*

Restart your adventure. Go back to 1.

DID YOU KNOW?

Wild horses live in herds. That's why, even when they live in an equestrian center, most horses prefer to be surrounded by many other horses.

14 Dr. Carol shakes her head. She thanks you for your honesty. However, she is very disappointed that you didn't read the book, especially when she had told you that to become a veterinarian, you have to study continuously to perfect your knowledge. Caring for horses and other animals is complex and difficult. You have to have lots of knowledge if you want to learn how to recognize illness and injury, and to make the right choices when it comes to treatment. You can't just make up veterinary care as you go along.
Unfortunately, you didn't listen to her advice and you didn't read the chapter about birth.

You don't have enough knowledge to help with the foal's birth, and Dr. Carol will not permit you to do so. You're just not serious enough to be her assistant.

You still earn 5 *points.*

Restart your adventure. Go back to 1 *.*

15 It's your turn. You mount your horse and steer him toward the main ring. The commentators announce your number, then the bell rings for you to enter the course.

It's the national competition and it demands a very high level of skill. The course is very difficult: there are tall jumps, wide jumps, and tight turns, so you have to be in harmony with your horse.

But from the beginning, you sense that something isn't right. Communicating with your horse isn't going well. The two of you aren't close enough and the course is too difficult for you. You knock down rails and your horse refuses a jump that is too high.

Your relationship with your horse is not strong enough: you haven't spent enough time together. You finish at the bottom of the class.

You still earn 5 *points.*

Restart your adventure. Go back to 1.

16 The nameplate on the door tells you that the sad horse is called Chocolate. The name is a perfect fit. His coat is a beautiful dark color that looks like dark chocolate, and his mane and tail are a creamy color, just like white chocolate. However, his head hangs down dejectedly at the back of his stall. He hasn't stuck his head out to see who's there and he hasn't even finished his food. He seems really depressed.

When he sees you enter his stall, he folds his ears back. When horses do this, it's a warning that they are not in a good mood.

If you want to pet Chocolate, go to 29.

If you'd rather keep your distance and speak to him softly, turn to 17.

17

You stay at the stall door to give Chocolate his space, because you don't want him to feel cornered. You speak to him with a gentle, calm voice to reassure him and let him know you mean him no harm. Horses are very sensitive to tone of voice. Even if they don't understand the words being spoken, they're able to understand what's being communicated to them based on tone.

After a few minutes, Chocolate's ears come forward. He's no longer in a bad mood; he's curious and attentive. Gradually, you win him over and he comes closer. Thanks to your patience and gentleness, Chocolate lets you pet him.

Well done. Continue to 6.

Did you know?

With eyes on the sides of their heads, horses have a wide field of vision. They can see 340°! By comparison, humans see around 180°. In other words, a horse can see from its left hip all the way to its right one.

18 Once the stables have been cleaned, Alex explains what a horse whisperer does. To become a whisperer, you have to learn to read a horse's body language, understand its reactions in nature, and learn to speak the same language. Whispering is communicating with horses in the language they themselves use in the wild. It requires lots of patience, observation, and sensitivity. You have to know how to put the horse's needs before your own.

Chocolate is very sad, because he lost his best friend. Horses form friendships that can last a lifetime, and separation is always very hard. However, thanks to horse whispering techniques, you can help him feel better and get happy again.

Continue to 12.

IT'S YOUR TURN!

Earn 3 points

In the grid below, circle the words associated with horse care and riding equipment. (Tip: Search these words on the internet once you're done to make sure you understand them.)

```
A W B R E A S T P L A T E
R I V E R B R U S H N E C
S O F T B R U S H E O R V
T H L E G E E F C A N C C
I A C H A L T E R S L A O
R C B L I N D E R I A C C
R K R E T U I R K R N U B
U A I R E S A D D L E R R
P M D B R I S T L E N R E
V O L A S N T S V O L Y E
C R E W S O R T W S O C C
K E N E L U I T E L U O H
T E O R I S T R R I S M I
C A N C O L L A R D I B N
V O L A E N T C A E N A G
C R U P P E R E E L U E C
T E O R I S T S R I S R V
```

GAITERS
HALTER
BLINDER
BRIDLE
SADDLE
CURRYCOMB
BRISTLE
BRUSH
SOFT BRUSH
STIRRUP
HACKAMORE
COLLAR
BREECHING
TRACES
BREASTPLATE
CRUPPER

19

You go shopping, because you want to buy a new outfit for the competition. It's your first horse show and you want to wear a really elegant riding jacket and breeches.
The day of the competition, you're the best dressed out of all the participants and everyone looks at you with envy.

However, you spent more time shopping than training, and your relationship with your horse suffered from it. Your course run does not go well. Your horse knocks down rails and even refuses a jump.

You finish near the bottom of the class, and you don't qualify for the national competition.

You still earn 5 *points.*

Restart your adventure. Go back to 1.

20 The horse's name is posted on the stall door. He's called Saffron and his coat is chestnut with tall white socks on three of his legs. He's very happy you've come to see him and he likes it when you scratch his withers. You get along really well with him. However, you notice that he has a bandage on his leg. Alex, the groom, explains that he was injured and he still has some healing to do before he can be ridden. He suggests you choose another horse.

If you want to meet the other horses, go to 2.

If you want to help the groom clean Saffron's leg, go to 27.

21 There's no magic spell to help a horse feel better, because each horse and each case is unique. You just have to be patient, listen, and observe. A horse can tell you itself what's wrong, if you can understand its language. The position of its ears, its head, its tail, and also the expression in its eyes, its nostrils, and its mouth are good signs to watch for.
With Alex's help, you manage to decipher Chocolate's body language. You understand that he needs company and encouragement, but also space. You have to be by his side, without smothering him.

If you want to sleep in his stall to be with him night and day, go to 13.

If you want to ride him, try 24.

If you'd rather take him out for a walk on foot, turn to 26.

? DID YOU KNOW?
The earliest horse known to science is called the Hyracotherium and lived 50 million years ago. It was tiny! No bigger than a goat or a deer.

22

You want to visit the stables first, because you can't wait to meet the horses. The stables are big, clean, and airy. Twenty or so stalls are lined up on each side. A stall is the enclosed space with a roof where horses live when they're not in the pasture. The ground is usually covered with straw or sawdust so it's more comfortable. Horses of all different sizes and colors stick their heads out in curiosity to watch you come in. They hope you have treats in your pockets. What do you want to do?

If you want to go see the horse that's neighing hello, go to 20.

If you'd rather go see the horse who stayed at the back of his stall looking sad, turn to 16.

? DID YOU KNOW?

Horses live on average 25 to 30 years and are fully grown at 5 or 6 years old. The record is held by a horse named Old Billy, who lived to the age of 62.

23 Birth is a magical moment, but it's also a delicate one. Therefore, you have to take precautions. A mare giving birth can be nervous, and she may defend herself if she feels in danger. A newborn foal is still fragile and sensitive. It's important to have certain knowledge when helping a veterinarian during a birth.
Dr. Carol looks you in the eye and asks you to answer honestly. At the end of the book she gave you, there was a whole chapter about horse pregnancy and birth. Did you read the whole book?

If you read the book yesterday afternoon, go to 10.

If you went to watch the circus parade, go to 14.

(If you can't remember, look at which one you circled back in 3)

IT'S YOUR TURN!

Earn 3 points

Here are the steps for making an origami horse. You too can create a paper horse!

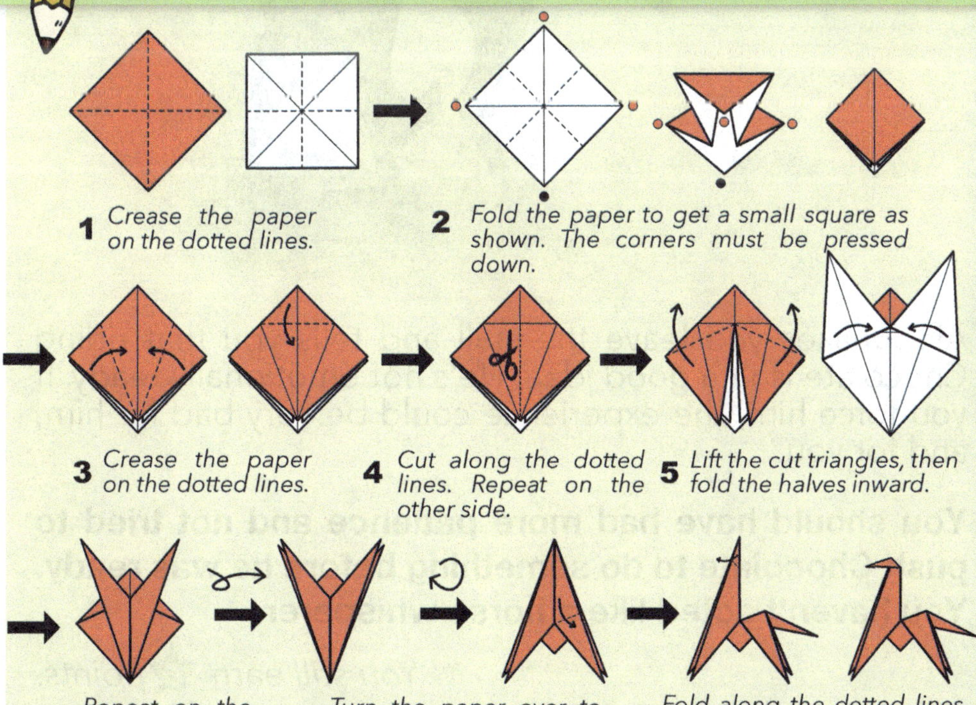

1 *Crease the paper on the dotted lines.*

2 *Fold the paper to get a small square as shown. The corners must be pressed down.*

3 *Crease the paper on the dotted lines.*

4 *Cut along the dotted lines. Repeat on the other side.*

5 *Lift the cut triangles, then fold the halves inward.*

6 *Repeat on the other side.*

7 *Turn the paper over to have the "legs" on the bottom.*

8 *Fold along the dotted lines and refold inward to create the horse's head and tail.*

If you have any trouble, ask an adult to help you watch an instructional video on the internet: search "origami horse."

24 You think that exercise will help Chocolate feel better. You get the saddle and bridle, but when you try to tack up, he retreats to the back of his stall, his ears folded down. You try to get close once again, but now he doesn't trust you. He doesn't want you to get any closer. He wants you to leave him alone.

Alex makes you leave the stall and tells you that riding Chocolate isn't a good idea. He's not emotionally ready. If you force him, the experience could be very bad for him, and for you.

You should have had more patience and not tried to push Chocolate to do something before he was ready. You haven't acted like a horse whisperer.

You still earn 5 *points.*

Restart your adventure. Go back to 1 .

25 Alex saw clearly that you weren't afraid of hard work when you helped him clean the stables. He tells Michael that you have a good heart and that you deserve the chance to try to help Chocolate. Michael takes a little time before coming to a decision.

With hard work, patience, and Alex's help, you get Chocolate used to living in the community again. He gradually relearns how to trust and allows other people to approach him. He even makes a new friend: a horse named Saffron.

Seeing this progress, Michael is very satisfied. He decides not to sell Chocolate. Your friend stays at the Little Gallop Equestrian Center and he rediscovers his happiness, thanks to you.

Thanks to your sensitivity and ability to listen, you got Chocolate to trust again. You understand his feelings better than anyone. You're worthy of the greatest of horse whisperers!

You earn 20 *points.*

But you can restart your adventure at 1 .

26 You decide to take Chocolate for a walk on foot. A breath of fresh air will do him good, and since you're not riding him, he can decide his own pace. You walk side by side for a long time. You occasionally scratch his withers. Sometimes he stops to have a bite of grass when there's a particularly appetizing tuft. Little by little, he relaxes and seems to enjoy the walk.

You sense that the moment has come! You whisper in Chocolate's ear and, feeling his approval, you step into a stirrup and climb up on his back! Congratulations. Chocolate has finally accepted you and you continue your stroll first at a walk, then a trot.

When you get back to the Equestrian Center, Chocolate seems tired, but changed! Alex is impressed: it's been a long time since he saw Chocolate so happy and relaxed. He believes the two of you make a good team, so he suggests you continue taking care of Chocolate.

If you want to teach Chocolate some tricks, go to 30.

Otherwise, you can go try out the jumping course. To do this, turn to 34.

27 Alex shows you how to clean Saffron's wound. It's very important to keep the wound clean so that it doesn't get worse. The disinfectant stings a bit, but Saffron is brave. You scratch his withers to help him keep his mind on other things. Saffron feels better thanks to your presence and your actions. He trusts you and you become friends.

A few days later, thanks to you and Alex, Saffron is doing better. However, the veterinarian still has to come examine him to make sure that everything is going well. While you wait, Alex asks if you'd like to help clean the stables. The stall bedding needs to be changed, the troughs cleaned, and the floors swept.

If you want to help Alex, go to 2.

Otherwise, you can go take the entrance exam for the jumping class at 31.

28 Michael, the owner of the Little Gallop Equestrian Center, is very impressed with Chocolate's progress. He didn't think the horse could improve so much. Plus, the tricks you taught him are so clever. However, he's decided to sell him. Even if Chocolate seems happy now that you're taking care of him, he continues to fold his ears back whenever someone other than you or Alex approaches him. The other day, he almost kicked a young rider.

Even if he's happy with you, a horse at the Equestrian Center must be comfortable around many different people. A horse that threatens to kick anyone who gets close cannot stay in an Equestrian Center.

If you helped Alex clean the stables, go to 25.

If you didn't help Alex, turn to 37.

(If you can't remember, check which one you circled back in 6)

29 Despite Chocolate's folded-back ears, you decide to get close enough to pet him. But Chocolate is really not in the mood. He turns around so you're faced with his hindquarters and he threatens to kick you if you come any closer. You run out of the stall to avoid getting hurt.

Horses are living creatures with emotions and moods just like you. They generally express these feelings though body language. To have a good relationship with a horse, you have to learn how to recognize these signs and respect the horse's feelings. If you try to force a horse rather than understand it and work together, it will react negatively, and neither the rider nor the horse will have a good experience.

You didn't read the signs that Chocolate was sending and you didn't respect his feelings. Next time, remember that the horse's well-being comes first!

You still earn 5 *points.*

Restart your adventure. Go back to 1 *.*

30 Chocolate is a very smart horse. He has a curious and playful nature, and he loves to learn new things. Some days, you go out for a walk together to get some fresh air, and other days, you try out new tricks. You gradually teach him how to bow, to shake and nod his head, and to do the Spanish walk. You even put on a little exhibition for the riders at the Little Gallop Equestrian Center.

Weeks pass and thanks to you and Alex, Chocolate is doing much better. He's eating again and has regained the weight he had lost. He's in good health and seems happy when you're looking after him.

Continue to 28.

31 You've reached the try-out lesson. It's time to test your knowledge. Answer these questions to find out if you can join the jumping class.

Jumping Class Entrance Exam

Question 1

How do you make a horse move?

A) Give it a little kick with your heel
B) Squeeze your legs against its flankss
C) Hit it with your crop

Question 2

Which of the following describes a horse's diet?

A) Carnivore
B) Omnivore
C) Herbivore

Question 3

What do you call a horse's coloration?

A) Its hair
B) Its coat color
C) Its complexion

Question 4

How can you tell what mood a horse is in?

A) By its ears
B) By its nostrils
C) By its mouth

Question 5

Which of these doesn't belong?

A) Helmet
B) Stirrups
C) Bit
D) Crop
E) Saddle
F) Hooves

Circle your answers:

Question 1) A - B - C
Question 2) A - B - C
Question 3) A - B - C
Question 4) A - B - C
Question 5) A - B - C - D - E - F

If you get less than 4 answers correct, go to 35.

Otherwise, turn to 34.

(The answer key can be found in 45)

32 Every horse at the Little Gallop Equestrian Center can do trail rides and rider training courses, but only a certain few can compete. Since you're going to be training for a jumping competition, you're going to need a horse that jumps well.
Lisa decides to pair you with Saffron. Saffron is a very good jumping horse and has already won several prizes. However, since he recently suffered an injured leg, even though he is now fully healed, he's going to need attention and training to be back at his best. It's up to you to figure out how to communicate with him and train together to achieve the best partnership possible.

If you want to train with Saffron to take part in the competition, go to 11.

If you'd rather help the veterinarian who treated Saffron, turn to 7.

33

You continue to train with your horse, since the national competition will soon be here. One day, Lisa tells you that a new horse is coming to the Little Gallop Equestrian Center. He's a champion horse who has already won many awards. He has even taken part in the national competition several times with other riders. He's very graceful when he jumps and he's as fast as the wind. He's really an exceptional horse.
He will arrive at the Equestrian Center a few days before the national competition, and Lisa suggests you ride him when you compete.

You can choose to ride the champion or else you can stick with the horse you've trained with

Ride the champion | ***Stick with your horse***

Then continue to 8.

DID YOU KNOW?

The world's tallest horse in recent years was 6 ft 10 in tall at the withers! His name was Big Jake and he weighed around 2500 pounds. That's the weight of a small car!

IT'S YOUR TURN!

Earn 3 points

Color in this beautiful day at the Equestrian Center.

34 Jumping requires lots of balance, responsiveness, and control. It's not a sport for beginners. First you have to know how to maintain good posture and how to steer your horse. Otherwise, you risk injury, both to yourself and your horse.
Lisa watches you ride during the try-out lesson. Unfortunately, she doesn't think you're advanced enough yet to join the jumping class.

But don't be sad – this is only temporary. Take riding lessons at the Equestrian Center so you can improve. With practice and perseverance, you can become the best rider and choose whatever aspect of horseback riding you like best.

Unfortunately, you could not join the jumping class.

You still earn 5 *points.*

Restart your adventure. Go back to 1 *.*

35 During the try-out lesson, Lisa first asks you to go over rails on the ground to test your balance and control. She then asks you to try cavaletti poles, and finally jumps. You like it a lot, because it's exciting and fun, like a roller coaster on horseback. The instructor can see that you're already a good rider and that you listen well to her guidance. You know how to maintain good posture and you communicate well with your horse. Lisa thinks you're advanced enough to join the jumping class.
Jumping is not easy, but it's very interesting. If you take training seriously, you'll be able to take part in horse shows and maybe win prizes.

Continue to 32.

IT'S YOUR TURN!

Earn 3 points

Complete the jumping course by going once and only once over each obstacle, only making only 4 straight lines. (In other words, connect the obstacles without lifting your pencil, making 4 straight lines that go once - and only once - through each obstacle.)

36 To reward your horse for his hard work, you brush him for a long time and give him a good massage. You even prepare him a mash, which is a mixture of boiled grains that refreshes a horse and helps it recuperate after hard work. You horse did so well at the competition and he deserves to be spoiled.

Brushing and grooming is a special time between a horse and a human. It lets you check in on your horse's health and develop your friendship.

If you have not yet become friends with your horse, you have now. Your bond strengthens.

(Record this in 44)

Continue to 33.

DID YOU KNOW?

Horses have a very particular digestive system. They are herbivores and have a very small stomach. They eat small quantities of food continuously, all day long. But be careful! Horses can't throw up, so you have to make sure they don't eat too much all at once. Otherwise, they could have quite the stomachache.

IT'S YOUR TURN!

Earn **3** *points*

Color in this beautiful scene with you and your horse.

37 Alex tells you that Michael is right. A nervous horse cannot stay at the Equestrian Center, because he could end up being a danger to inexperienced riders who don't understand horses' body language. It's an accident waiting to happen. Without a doubt, Chocolate would be better off in a private stable with only one person to ride him.

Michael really likes Chocolate and he doesn't want to sell him to just anyone. He finds a good family that understands how to communicate with Chocolate and will take good care of him.

However, the family lives far away, and you'll no longer be able to see Chocolate. You're sad, and Chocolate is too.

You still earn 5 *points.*

Restart your adventure. Go back to 1 .

38 Alex tells Dr. Carol that not only did you volunteer to help him clean Saffron's wound, but you also managed to become friends with him and helped him stay calm. Alex also says that after having helped out with Saffron's care, you then helped him clean the whole stables. You have a big heart and you work hard. He's very proud to have someone like you at the Little Gallop Equestrian Center because you're really passionate about it.

Dr. Carol pushes her glasses back onto her nose and smiles at you. When she smiles, she looks really kind. Convinced by everything Alex said, she lets you assist her.

Continue to 5.

IT'S YOUR TURN!

Earn 3 points

Before starting your adventure with Dr. Carol, let's review horse anatomy! Connect the following words with the numbers on the diagram:

Breast, Fetlock, Mane, Neck, Croup, Tail, Withers, Hoof, Nostril

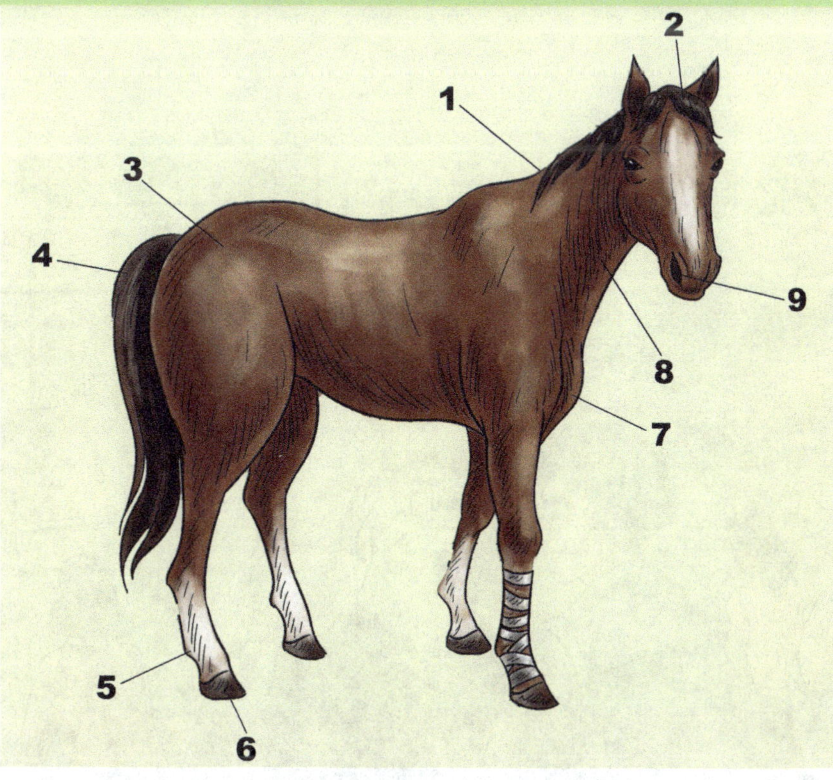

39 You and your horse have trained with dedication. You now have a very good relationship. By the day of the competition, you both feel ready.

You have a really good run. Your horse doesn't knock down a single rail and doesn't dodge or refuse any jumps. You commit no faults. Two other riders do the same, but you are the pair that completed the course the fastest. You win the competition.

Lisa congratulates you. She's so happy that your work has paid off and she lets you know that you've qualified for the national championships!

If you want to leave your horse with the groom to go celebrate your victory, go to 33.

If you want to groom your horse yourself, turn to 36.

40 The next day, as you're leaving school, you run into Dr. Carol. She gives you some great news: Cinnamon, a mare at the Little Gallop Equestrian Center, is about to give birth. A foal will soon be born!
When it is born, a foal is able to stand up within just a few hours. Foals have to learn to stand quickly, because in the wild, horses are prey. The best way they know to defend themselves is by galloping off as quickly as possible. That's also why foals are born with such long legs.
In the wild, mares give birth alone, but there are sometimes complications. A veterinarian makes sure everything goes right and helps the mare if she needs it.

Continue to 23.

? DID YOU KNOW?

Mares carry their foals for 11 months. Therefore, horses have a longer gestation period than humans.

41 The time has come: it's your turn. You get in the saddle and enter the main ring. Your horse is as impatient as you are to start the course. You have a deep connection. The course is difficult, but you have confidence in your horse and your own abilities. You've trained well and you've been through a lot together. Nothing can stop you now.

You set off. You don't jump over the obstacles, you fly! You pass every obstacle without a hitch and you finish your run without any faults. It's the fastest run of the whole competition.

Thanks to your relationship based in trust, your dedication, and your harmony, you win first place in the Big Show. Congratulations! You're a Grand Rider!

You earn 20 *points.*

But you can restart your adventure at 1 .

42 TEST YOUR KNOWLEDGE

Complete this quiz at the end of your adventure. To find the right answers, pay attention to the "Did you know?" sections as you read.

1 **A mare can have several pregnancies a year.**
True or False?

2 **Horses are carnivores and eat mostly meat.**
True or False?

3 **Horses are solitary creatures, which is why they prefer to be isolated in stalls.**
True or False?

4 **A horse whisperer:**
A) Takes care of and retrains horses by understanding their needs.
B) Can steer horses by voice.
C) Is a mute horse that can't neigh.

5 **A horse's height is measured:**
A) At the head. B) At the withers. C) At the flank.

6 **What do you feed a horse to help it regain its strength:**
A) Mash. B) Straw. C) Treats.

7 **What does it mean when a horse folds back its ears?**
A) That it's sick. B) That it's happy.
C) That it's in a bad mood.

8 **A horse will throw up when it eats too much.**
True or False?

→ Check your answers in 45 and record your points in 43.

43 RECORD YOUR POINTS HERE

Whenever you score a point during your adventure, color in the corresponding star. When they have all been colored, you can finally claim the title of **Grand Rider, Friend of the Horses.**

20 20 20

5 5 5
5 5 5
5 5 5

3 3 3 3
3 3 3 3
3 3 3 3
3 3 3 3

Add up your points to find out where you are in the adventure!

(You can ask an adult for help if it's too difficult.)

Grand Rider
Friend of the Horses

Congratulations, you are now an exceptional rider. Your victories are many, the horses love you, and you are renowned by all as the most talented of the riders.

153

Grand Rider

You've now advanced to **Grand Rider!** In addition to mastering the perfect technique, you are sensitive to the horses' needs. You understand their emotions and become one with them. You're worthy of the greatest of

120

Experienced Rider

Way to go! You now have the stuff of an **experienced rider.** You've mastered jumping and you're even teaching your horse some tricks. Horseback riding is truly your passion.

80

Young Rider

You're gaining experience and learning quickly. You now know how to mount a horse, how to trot and gallop. You've also learned how to clean the stables. You're on the right path, **young rider!**

40

Budding Rider

You've barely begun the story! You don't even know how to brush a horse yet, and you're afraid to step in any droppings. Continue your training, **budding rider!**

44 FRIEND OF THE HORSES?

Throughout your adventure, if you make the right choices and take good care of your horse, you can become its friend. That means that you've formed a strong bond based in trust. Record it here when you reach the marker:

☐ **You and your horse have become «friends.»**

SOLUTIONS

45 ANSWERS AND SOLUTIONS

ANSWER KEY FOR 42

1 - False 2 - False 3 - False 4 - A) 5 - B)
6 - A) 7 - C) 8 - False

ACTIVITY SOLUTIONS

Activity 1

Crossword

1 → Rider
2 → Horseshoe
3 → Canter
4 → Bit
5 → Riding Ring
6 → Stirrup
7 → Forelock
8 → Trot
9 → Straw
10 → Chestnut

Activity 4

Sudoku

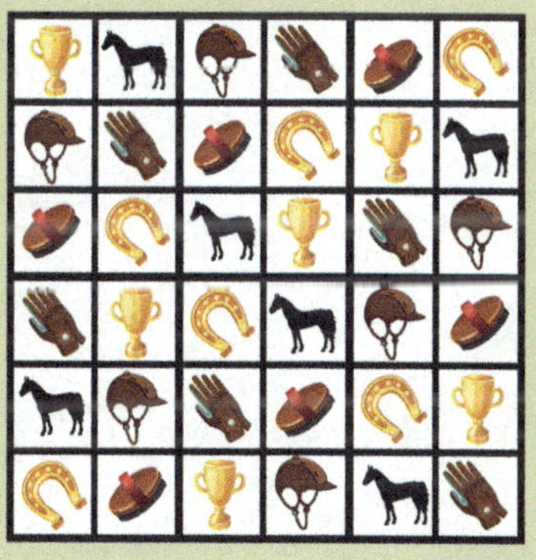

Activity 18

Activity 35

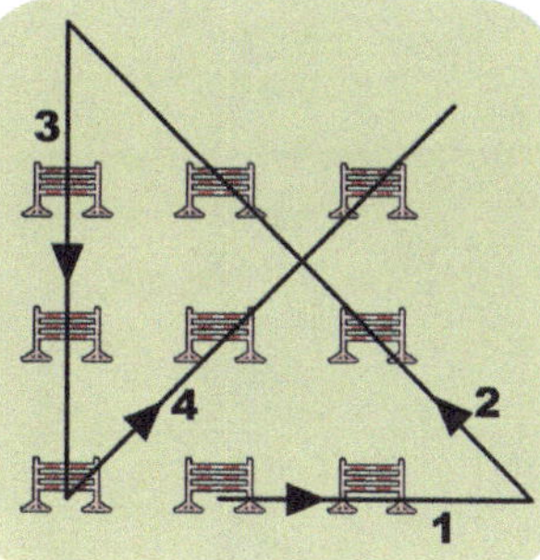

Activity 38

1 – Withers
2 – Mane
3 – Croup
4 – Tail
5 – Fetlock
6 – Hoof
7 – Breast
8 – Neck
9 – Nostril

ANSWER KEY FOR THE ENTRANCE EXAM IN 31

Question 1 - A
Question 2 - C
Question 3 - B
Question 4 - A
Question 5 - F

Bonus Colorings

Made in the USA
Coppell, TX
27 November 2023

24652281R00044